THE CARAVAN GALLERY

IS BRITAIN GREAT? 3

Sign of the Times
Sara-Jayne Parsons

I've passed by the Wellington Pub on Picton Road in Liverpool regularly for several years now and it's become a significant coordinate on my internal daily map. The pub's bottle green and rust-red tile facade adorned with a ubiquitous SKY Sports banner is unremarkable, but the sign above the door - Locally Known Affectionally as "The Welly" - is unforgettable. I smile every time I catch a glimpse of it for a number of reasons. It locates my home; not just in its proximity to the actual bricks-and-mortar of the place where I live, but also the wider geography of the city I love.

The sign sounds better in Scouse, an accent where frequently words are shortened with "ly" creating an informal quality to what is being said. In this case, the colloquial familiarity used to describe "The Welly" suggests it's a comfortable, friendly place, beloved and valued by the surrounding neighbourhood. The sign bestows a recognised value on an unexceptional place and it reminds me of photographs by Jan Williams and Chris Teasdale that I've seen in The Caravan Gallery; images of contemporary Britain which highlight juxtapositions of language and location sometimes resulting in humorous or ironic new meanings.

Williams and Teasdale have photographed in Liverpool numerous times in recent years and I've been privileged to get to know them as they've explored the streets at a time of great change in the city. One of the most memorable images they captured during this time is of a grotty, rundown shop (not that far from "The Welly" as it happens) depicting a handwritten sign that reads "Sunbeds English Lessons." It's the incongruity of the two activities that strikes the viewer first. Do you get both services at the same time? Now that would be an efficient combination, although the exterior of the shop doesn't suggest anything very modern in the way of treatments or convenience. And what does this shop's very specific provision reveal about its targeted customer, located as it is in a working class area undergoing regeneration, comprised predominantly of immigrant families and students?

Such photographs expose the power of Williams and Teasdale's simple phenomenological observations and efforts to capture the spirit of place; their vernacular images are a semiotic frame through which to consider how people identify themselves and their environment, as they navigate their everyday lives. Sometimes their photographs highlight eccentricities of daily life; they isolate garish juxtapositions of colour, pattern and texture for formal study akin to the aesthetic coolness found in the work of other practitioners of the everyday such as Martin Parr. At other times their camera becomes a tool to raise awareness about difficult issues found in the contemporary landscape; the work of John Davies springs to mind in this regard.

Either way, Williams and Teasdale don't set out to proselytize. Their mission isn't moral but rather to record the ordinary and extraordinary, and to document contemporary life as they find it. The territory of their lens is typically places that are in transition; urban areas slated for regeneration or reinvention, or liminal neighbourhoods between the city centre and traditionally suburban areas. In another century their work might be aligned with efforts of the original Mass Observation photographers and their attempts to create a visual archive of ordinary life in Britain. Indeed Williams and Teasdale are not so interested in the wealthy elite or the newly squeezed middle of the Lib-Dem-Con Coalition, but rather their focus is on the already squashed and marginalised lower end of British society.

However, unlike Mass Observation efforts, humour plays a significant and reoccurring role in Williams and Teasdale's astute social and cultural comment. It's a strategy historically associated with political satire in visual art which remains effective, and the photographers recognise this. For example, it could be said that their approach proffers a respectful nod to William Hogarth's examination of 18th century urban living. Like his prints and drawings, their photographs are simultaneously seductive and analytical, resulting in a type of visual stand-up routine that celebrates and critiques contemporary life. And similar to the very best of observational comedy which becomes political satire, the humour expressed through their images pulls the viewer in to contemplate reality in sharper critical focus.

The success and popularity of The Caravan Gallery rests on this capacity, which is supported by the very nature of how Williams and Teasdale work. They make several research visits to locations they are interested in or have read about in news reports. But more often than not their itineraries are made up of places recommended when talking to people on location or following local gossip; the vernacular nature of their photographs corresponds to their colloquial research. Their resulting photographs are not made from a high-horse or cool objective position.

Against the backdrop of photographic exhibitions, The Caravan Gallery becomes a discursive space that seems at home anywhere it's parked up, whether, in my experience, the rather grand vista of the Bluecoat's courtyard or the car park at the Asda on Smithdown Road, L15. The modest and inviting character of the Caravan is matched by the warm welcome offered by Williams and Teasdale as you enter. They are accessible, generous and non-judgemental which makes curious visitors feel comfortable when asking questions, sharing stories or suggesting places to photograph.

In this instance The Caravan Gallery becomes a sort of neighbourhood TripAdvisor; a place for research and reviews by and for people who like visual travels. And it follows that this rich, inclusive, participatory way of making photographs on location ensures that wherever they go, Williams and Teasdale are most definitely "locally known affectionally."

Sara-Jayne Parsons
Exhibitions Curator, the Bluecoat
Liverpool, October 2011

IN SEARCH OF THE PERFECT IMAGE
Dan Thompson

There have been two great creators of British postcards. Two who not only mass-produced 15 by 21cm photographic images on cheap card, but also defined how we see ourselves as a nation.

The first was John Hinde, originally a photographer for the Civil Defence during the Second World War. While Raphael Tuck produced the first colour postcards in Britain, it was from the mid-1950s that Hinde's company turned up the colour and consequently sold Britain to the world. Hinde's images, at first glance snapshots of British life, are in fact carefully composed. Clean beaches and wholesome families, iconic buildings and red buses, ancient history and the latest fashions. Britain with the bad bits taken out.

Hinde had previously taken to the road with his own travelling show, a circus company touring Ireland. When he returned to photography, he used large format cameras and the latest film, and a special Italian printing process that saturated his cards with vivid colour. He captured not British life, but an airbrushed, spritzed up, ersatz, heritage reproduction of it.

The second great producer of postcards is The Caravan Gallery, a pairing of photographers Jan Williams and Chris Teasdale, brought together through a sunshine yellow caravan converted into a mobile art gallery in 2000. Like Hinde, they have toured the UK in search of The Perfect Image, stopping to explore every town and city along the way. They have become experts in the minutiae of British life, and can find you the cheapest coffee in Coventry, recommend the best butcher in Brixton, show you the secondhand shops of Shoreham by Sea and tell you why you might want to avoid a B&B in Carlisle's Botchergate district. They're connoisseurs of plastic cutlery, supermarket cuisine and bargains from Britain's markets.

Like Hinde, they have found a mass market for their work, selling picture postcards, books and calendars in galleries and bookshops and from their caravan as they travel. Like Hinde, they have wholeheartedly embraced new technology from the outset with various computers, Panasonic Lumix G series cameras and now a large format Hewlett Packard printer.

Unlike Hinde, they're not interested in the glossy or polished; they're after the grit and grime, the detail and fine grain. Where he turned up the colour, they turn up the grey. Where he saw clean beaches, they see the car park next to them. Where he saw heritage architecture, they see the gift shop. Where he saw the sparkling blue rivers of middle England, they see sluggish streams full of urban litter. And not in a knowing, ironic, slightly sneering way either; they have a genuine love for this stuff that's left at the side.

Of course, the postcard is a convenient and accessible medium, but there's much more to The Caravan Gallery than that. Williams and Teasdale are master street photographers, pursuing Gilbert & George's manifesto in search of art that will speak across the barriers of knowledge directly to People about their Life and not about their knowledge of art. Take their images away from the postcards, print them large and frame them expensively, hang them in a clean white space and it's a magnificent body of work.

Like Gilbert & George, Williams and Teasdale are performance artists as well as photographers. The Caravan Gallery isn't really the white gallery space it pretends to be, it's a theatre for the dozens of encounters its artists stage wherever they stop. It's a studio to record real life, capture the locally distinct, preserve the true and best of British as it's found. And what a record - tens of thousands of images make up an unrivalled social history of the start of the 21st century.

The Caravanners are recorders, psychogeographers, exploring spaces and the edges of places as they try to find what make them interesting by capturing every detail. And they're visionaries, extolling the virtues of a way of living and uncovering the truth. Spend time with them - whether looking at their books, collecting their postcards or visiting the caravan itself - and you'll start to see the world the way they do.

Sitting in a beach hut on Worthing seafront writing this in the early morning sun I'm aware of ragged cloud, ever shifting pebbles and drifts of tamarisk trees, but I'm more interested in fat ladies on shopping bikes, tired tattooed joggers, superfluous signposts and blue building site fences. The Caravan Gallery gets inside your head, and shows you that all of this is great.

Dan Thompson
Empty Shops Network
http://www.artistsandmakers.com

TABLOID BRITAIN

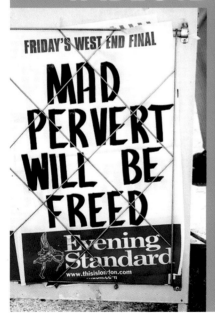

Cover Images
Front Cover - Tilbury
Inside front cover - Needham Market
Inside back cover - Needham Market

Former holiday park, Portsmouth

Monkey World Tank Museum, Wareham

Southend

Holiday Chalets, Sheppey

Travellers at Billy Banks, Penarth

Chalet Park, Sheppey

Holiday Park, Sheppey

Coventry

Birmingham

Hastings Pier (details of restoration campaign at www.hpwrt.co.uk)

Grays Beach, Essex

Shopping at Sheerness beach, Sheppey

Beach on first floor, Liverpool One Shopping Centre

Southsea

Salcombe

Royal Wedding Day at Gunwharf Quays, Portsmouth

Liverpool

Saturday afternoon, Liverpool

Chelmsford

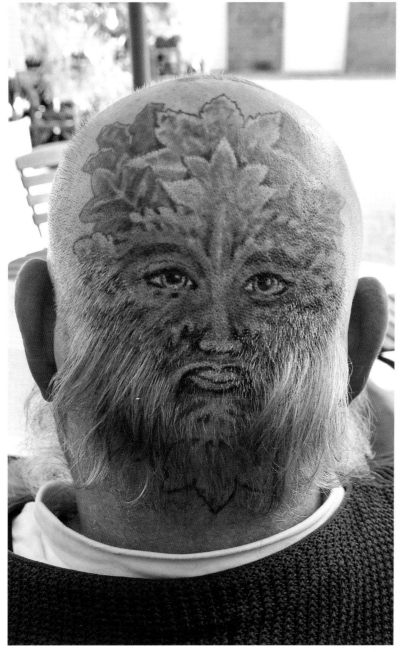

Mottisfont

Portsmouth

Dalston, London

Euston, London

Walsall

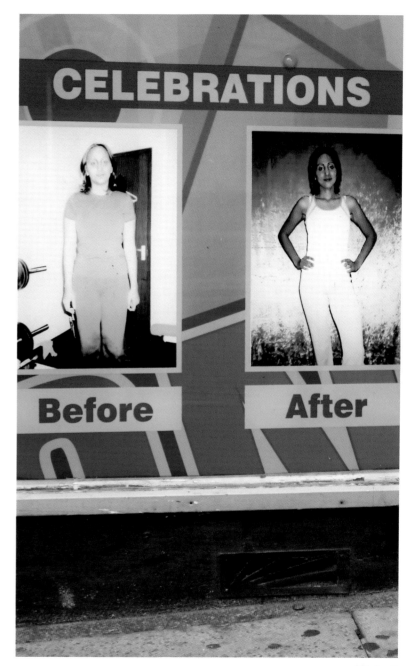

Walsall

Derby

Grays

Macclesfield

Sittingbourne

Hair salon, Dalston, London

Stoke Newington, London

Bath

Southend

Cambridge

Leigh Park, Havant

Liverpool

FREEDOM IS
IN PERIL

DEFEND IT
WITH ALL
YOUR MIGHT

Bath

Stamford Hill, London

Liverpool

Faversham

Guildford

Wimbledon Chase, London

Pub window, Portsmouth

Formerly The Grave Diggers, Southsea

Formerly The Strand Bar, Southsea

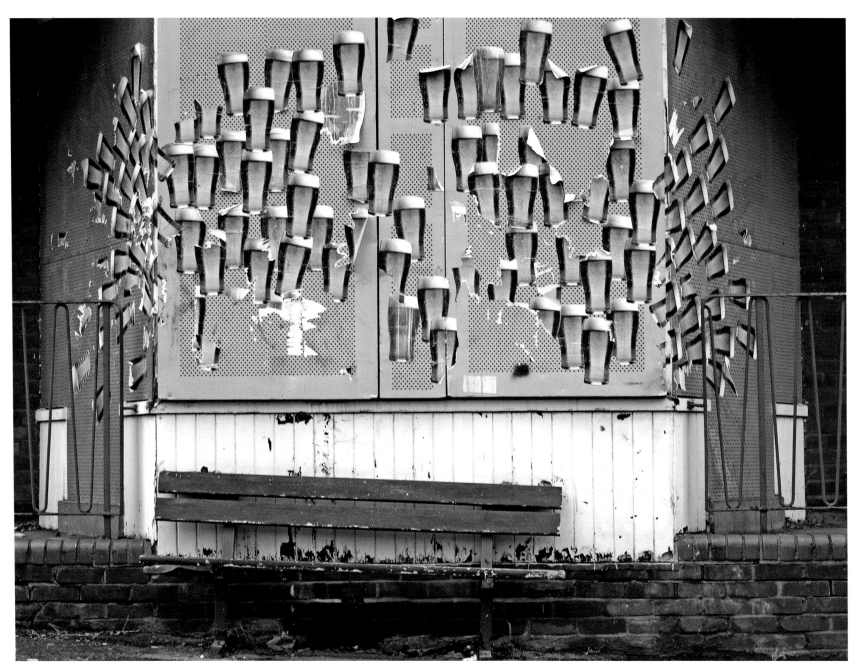

Hand in Hand Pub, Elephant and Castle, London

Pub garden, Portsmouth

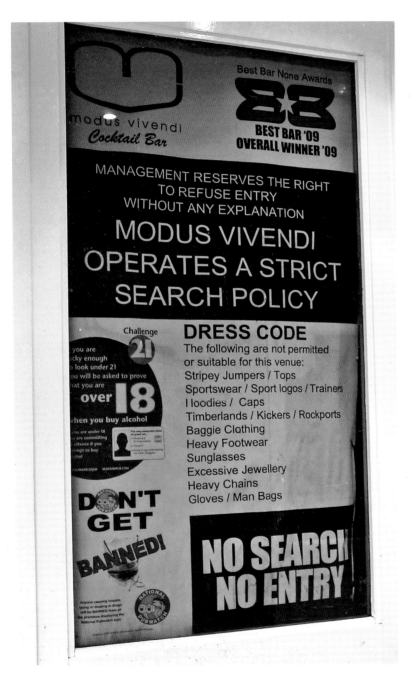

Walsall

Rochester

Portsmouth

West Bromwich

Southend

KIDDIES CORNER

All Served with Small Chips & Peas or Beans

CHILD FISH FINGER MEAL	£2.85
CHILD CHICKEN NUGGETS	£2.85
CHILD SAUSAGE	£2.85
CHILD BURGER	£2.85

EXTRA

EXTRA

EXTRA

Portion of

Peas, Bake
& Egg

Bread & B

Bognor Regis

Menu options, Grays

Transport Cafe, Guyhirn

Meal, Fratton style

Summer goodness, Stockport

Sittingbourne

Scotch Pies, Edinburgh

Silver lidded condiments, Salcombe

Cream tea, Bath

Portsmouth

Porthcawl

Elvis special, Porthcawl

Paul McCartney cake, Crosby

Chelmsford

Brighton

Salcombe

Public art, Walsall

Trolley dash from Asda, Portsmouth

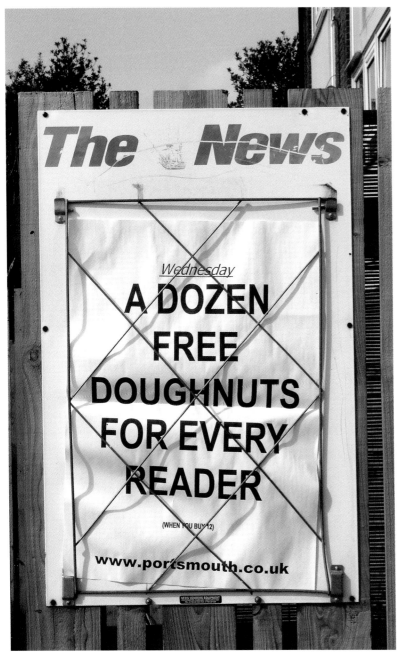

March 2008

August 2010

Just a note to let you know that whilst in your Bathroom, Customers at Asda's can see you naked.

Note posted through letterbox, Fratton

Bognor Regis

Shop display, Swanage

Stoke Newington, London

Gravesend

Tilbury

Tilbury

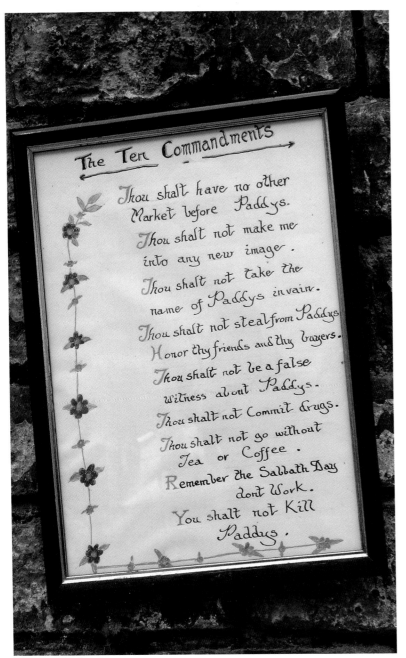

Paddy's market (deceased), Glasgow

Looking for love, Whitstable

Off licence, Emsworth

Portsmouth

West End, London

Fratton

Portsmouth

Bognor Regis

Thurrock

Liverpool

Dover

The Harrow, Steep

Private garden, Old Portsmouth

Walled garden, Portsmouth

Regal lion, Sheppey

Sheerness, Sheppey

Good News House, Salford

Greyhound stadium, Portsmouth

Guyhirn Lay-by Sit-in Transport Cafe, A47

Penarth

Farm shop, Wyre

Leigh Park, Havant

Stamford Hill balconies, London

Edinburgh

South Kilburn, London

South Kilburn, London

Gilfach Goch, Rhondda

Port Talbot

Tooting, London

Sittingbourne

Chelmsford

Hackney, London

Stonehenge

Hayling Island

Salcolme

One of Liverpool's 'Welsh Streets'

FOR SALE/TO LET
DEVELOPMENT OPPORTUNITY
PLANNING CONSENT FOR
60 APARTMENTS
0.14 HECTARES (0.35 ACRES)
POTENTIAL FOR SHORT TERM CAR
PARKING & ADVERTISING HOARDINGS

Anglican Cathedral, Liverpool

Ocean Terminal viewed from Asda car park, Leith, Edinburgh

Picton Regeneration Zone, Liverpool

Battersea Reach and coal quay, London viewed from the Thames Path by Sainsbury's (on the site of Fulham Power Station)

Pier Head area regeneration, Liverpool

Garston, Liverpool

Edge Hill, Liverpool

Moving On...

We've come a long way since our first outing to Southsea seafront in 2000. The Caravan Gallery Millennium Experience was to be a one-off public art installation commissioned by Art Space Portsmouth for August Bank Holiday weekend. A caravan seemed the perfect vehicle for an exhibition about leisure, landscape and lifestyle in Britain, ideal for taking art to the people and involving them in our enquiries.

Since that time we've travelled thousands of miles and exhibited in hundreds of locations across the UK and abroad, exploring sense of place and documenting the reality and surreality of 'the way we live today'. We've always liked to mix things up a bit and have appeared at community events in fields, petting farms, supermarket car parks, art galleries (inside and out) and street festivals. We've parked outside Tate Britain, London, Asda, Liverpool and Paul Smith, Tokyo, been invited to biennials and photography festivals (including one in Guernsey where caravans are banned) and met people from all walks of life.

Wherever we are The Caravan Gallery takes on the role of miniature social club and confession box on wheels. Everyone can relate to photos. They get people talking, laughing and sometimes crying. Some people are primarily concerned with the aesthetics of an image whereas others focus on the story behind a picture - needless to say we're interested in both. Before exhibiting in a location we'll make a research trip to take pictures and get a feel for a place. Our radar for local distinctiveness, current trends, oddness and absurdity is pretty well tuned after years of exploration but we don't always realise the significance of what we're looking at the time. This is where our audience comes in. We find people love recognising places and sharing background information, some of which is really quite bizarre. Conversely it frequently happens that we display a photo of something that caught our eye only to find out that local residents were totally unaware of its existence. They tell us they'll start looking around them a bit more in future and resolve to carry a camera with them at all times 'just in case'.

We've always encouraged visitors to our exhibitions to express their views on contemporary Britain and tell us about their own lives. They share what they love and hate about places in specially devised Caravan Gallery surveys and frequently recommend 'photogenic' sights in our visitors' books.

Increasingly we're breaking out of the caravan and inhabiting empty shops, village halls, museums and galleries. We particularly enjoy projects where we can fully realise the potential for interaction and public participation.

Earlier this year we ran our first Pride of Place Project at the University of Portsmouth's Space Gallery. Half the exhibition consisted of our own photos and video portraits of local residents and visitors to the city. The rest of the show was created by the people who came along; they filled in surveys, brought photos and artefacts, wrote poems, made postcards and souvenirs and helped us create an amazingly anarchic and curiously entertaining People's Map of Portsmouth. We've since taken elements of this project on the road and adapted them to events in Guernsey, Liverpool and more recently Belgium where we were invited to participate in Kunst&Zwalm, 'an outdoor route with contemporary art'. Our hosts were slightly nervous that we wouldn't find anything to interest us in the peaceful rural landscape of the Flemish Ardennes, accustomed as we are to urban squalor, but we gradually warmed to the challenge and ended up feeling inspired to the point of obsession. Local people, curious to see how we saw perceived their environment, were happy to participate and we came away feeling confident that our concept can travel anywhere.

Our enthusiasm for exploring places and documenting the times in which we live remains undiminished and our observations and activities continue to find new outlets. The current financial climate (when every city wants to appear culturally vibrant but can't or won't pay for art) has forced many artists, ourselves included, to diversify and take the initiative (that's how The Caravan Gallery came into being after all). After years of talking about it we've finally teamed up with Dan Thompson of the Empty Shops Network to create Culture on Wheels, an international network for mobile arts projects, and are planning a number of festivals in 2012.

We're still drawn to the same tragicomic subject matter – the disparity between dreams and reality, weird juxtapositions, dereliction, stagnation and regeneration, the language of marketing and tourism and definitions of what is deemed picturesque. We've come across imaginative and successful attempts at regeneration as well as many examples of aspiration gone wrong. More often than not the most fascinating places we've found are a crazy combination of the two. Trends and fortunes come and go but we meet plenty of inspirational individuals who believe in turning negatives into positives. Economic recession is responsible for a whole range of problems but it's true to say that necessity is the mother of invention and gives rise to ingenious and maverick solutions.

Jan Williams and Chris Teasdale

www.thecaravangallery.co.uk
Facebook: The Caravan Gallery; Twitter: @caravangallery

The Caravan Gallery: Pride of Place Project, Space Gallery, University of Portsmouth

Artists' acknowledgements

We would like to thank everyone who has taken an interest in our work and supported us over the years — family, friends, funders, festival organisers, followers, facilitators and fans, especially those who bought our other *'Is Britain Great?'* books, making possible the publication of this third volume.

Contributors:
Many thanks to Sara-Jayne Parsons, Dan Thompson and Daniel Meadows for their invaluable contributions which give an added personal slant to our work.

PPG
As usual we are much obliged to our printers for their service, care and attention to detail. It makes a real difference having printers we can rely on.

Hewlett Packard
HP has provided us with a large format printer which means we can print up to A1 archival prints of unbelievable quality and longevity for exhibitions and sales.

Drobo
At last! A simple, safe device for sharing and backing up our hundreds of thousands of files courtesy of Drobo.

Panasonic
We are delighted that Panasonic is still providing us with the latest generation Micro 4/3 Lumix G cameras which are now producing even better quality still images and video. Being small and light they make ideal travelling companions.

First published in the United Kingdom in 2011 by Cornerhouse in association with The Caravan Gallery.

ISBN 978-0-9569571-0-8

Distributed worldwide by Cornerhouse Publications
www.cornerhouse.org/books
publications@cornerhouse.org

Photography: The Caravan Gallery

Design: The Caravan Gallery

Print: PPG Design & Print, Portsmouth
www.ppgprint.co.uk

R.I.P. PPG Robin

Cornerhouse
70 Oxford Street
Manchester M1 5NH
United Kingdom
www.cornerhouse.org

New-Generation System Cameras